ALL AROUND THE WORLD
BULGARIA

by Kristine Spanier, MLIS

pogo

Ideas for Parents and Teachers

Pogo Books let children practice reading informational text while introducing them to nonfiction features such as headings, labels, sidebars, maps, and diagrams, as well as a table of contents, glossary, and index.

Carefully leveled text with a strong photo match offers early fluent readers the support they need to succeed.

Before Reading

- "Walk" through the book and point out the various nonfiction features. Ask the student what purpose each feature serves.
- Look at the glossary together. Read and discuss the words.

Read the Book

- Have the child read the book independently.
- Invite him or her to list questions that arise from reading.

After Reading

- Discuss the child's questions. Talk about how he or she might find answers to those questions.
- Prompt the child to think more. Ask: Ships move goods along the Danube River. Can you think of other ways to move goods from one place to another?

Pogo Books are published by Jump!
5357 Penn Avenue South
Minneapolis, MN 55419
www.jumplibrary.com

Copyright © 2023 Jump!
International copyright reserved in all countries. No part of this book may be reproduced in any form without written permission from the publisher.

Library of Congress Cataloging-in-Publication Data

Names: Spanier, Kristine, author.
Title: Bulgaria / by Kristine Spanier, MLIS.
Description: Minneapolis, MN: Jump!, Inc., [2023]
Series: All around the world | Includes index.
Audience: Ages 7-10
Identifiers: LCCN 2022019728 (print)
LCCN 2022019729 (ebook)
ISBN 9798885241885 (hardcover)
ISBN 9798885241892 (paperback)
ISBN 9798885241908 (ebook)
Subjects: LCSH: Bulgaria–Juvenile literature.
Classification: LCC DR55 .S66 2023 (print)
LCC DR55 (ebook)
DDC 949.9–dc23/eng/20220429
LC record available at https://lccn.loc.gov/2022019728
LC ebook record available at https://lccn.loc.gov/2022019729

Editor: Jenna Gleisner
Designer: Molly Ballanger

Photo Credits: Todor Stoyanov/Shutterstock, cover; Valentin Valkov/Shutterstock, 1; Pixfiction/Shutterstock, 3; Nataliya Nazarova/Shutterstock, 4; Wirestock Creators/Shutterstock, 5; Atanas Paskalev/Dreamstime, 6-7; Sanga Park/iStock, 8-9; Martin Procházka/Dreamstime, 10-11tl; Andriy Nekrasov/iStock, 10-11tr; Roland Seitre/Minden Pictures/SuperStock, 10-11bl; Konstantin Mikhailov/Nature Picture Library, 10-11br; praetorianphoto/iStock, 12; Pani Garmyder/Shutterstock, 13; trabantos/Shutterstock, 14-15; etorres/Shutterstock, 16 (tarator); em-m/iStock, 16 (musaka); Mahlebashieva/Shutterstock, 16 (banitsa); Roy Conchie/Alamy, 17; Julian Popov/Shutterstock, 18-19; Wojtek BUSS /Gamma-Rapho/Getty, 20-21; johan10/iStock, 23.

Printed in the United States of America at Corporate Graphics in North Mankato, Minnesota.

TABLE OF CONTENTS

CHAPTER 1
By the Black Sea...4

CHAPTER 2
Life in Bulgaria..12

CHAPTER 3
Food and Fun...16

QUICK FACTS & TOOLS
At a Glance...22
Glossary..23
Index...24
To Learn More...24

CHAPTER 1

BY THE BLACK SEA

Would you like to see a **fortress**? You can in Bulgaria! Belogradchik Fortress is **ancient**. It was built from the 100s to 300s. Large rocks rise near it. They helped protect the fortress from enemies.

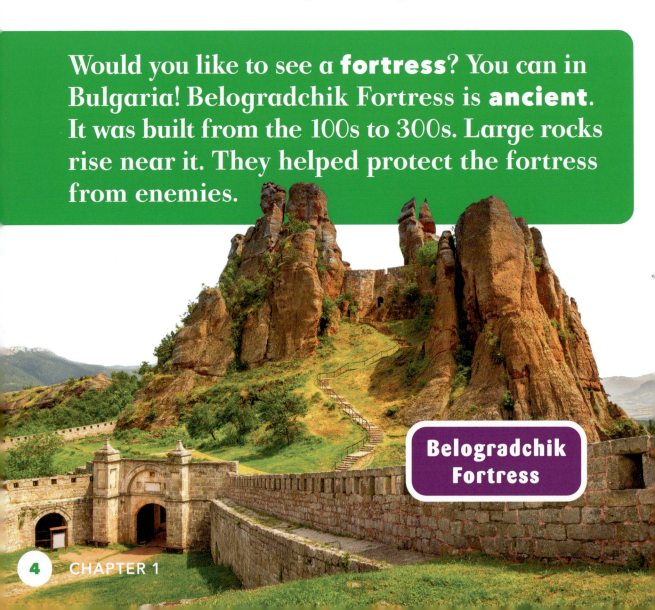

Belogradchik Fortress

Bulgaria is in southeastern Europe. The Black Sea is to the east. Nessebar is on the coast. This city is more than 3,000 years old!

Black Sea

CHAPTER 1

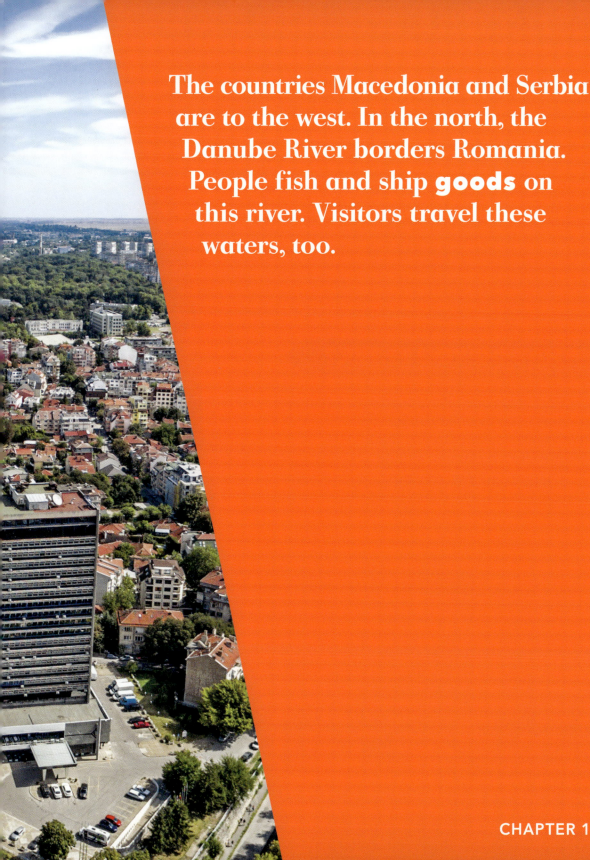

The countries Macedonia and Serbia are to the west. In the north, the Danube River borders Romania. People fish and ship **goods** on this river. Visitors travel these waters, too.

Plovdiv is near the center of Bulgaria. People have lived in this city for more than 8,000 years. It is known as the City of the Seven Hills. Why? Seven hills once stood here.

WHAT DO YOU THINK?

Rock from one hill in Plovdiv was used to build roads. Six hills remain. Do you think the city's nickname should change? Why or why not?

red deer

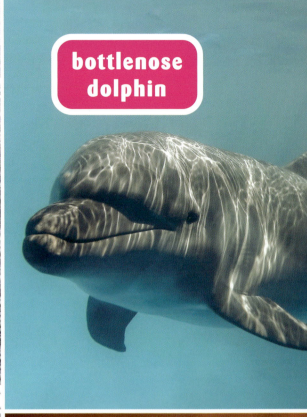
bottlenose dolphin

marbled polecat

gray dwarf hamster

The Rhodope Mountains are in the south. Red deer run through them. Bottlenose dolphins swim in the Black Sea. Marbled polecats dig underground. Gray dwarf hamsters hide in meadows.

WHAT DO YOU THINK?

Bottlenose dolphin numbers are declining. Why? **Pollution** is one reason. Do you think the government should protect them? Why or why not?

CHAPTER 1 | 11

CHAPTER 2
LIFE IN BULGARIA

Bulgarian students bring flowers to their teachers on the first day of school. After eighth grade, students take exams to get into high school. They finish high school by age 16.

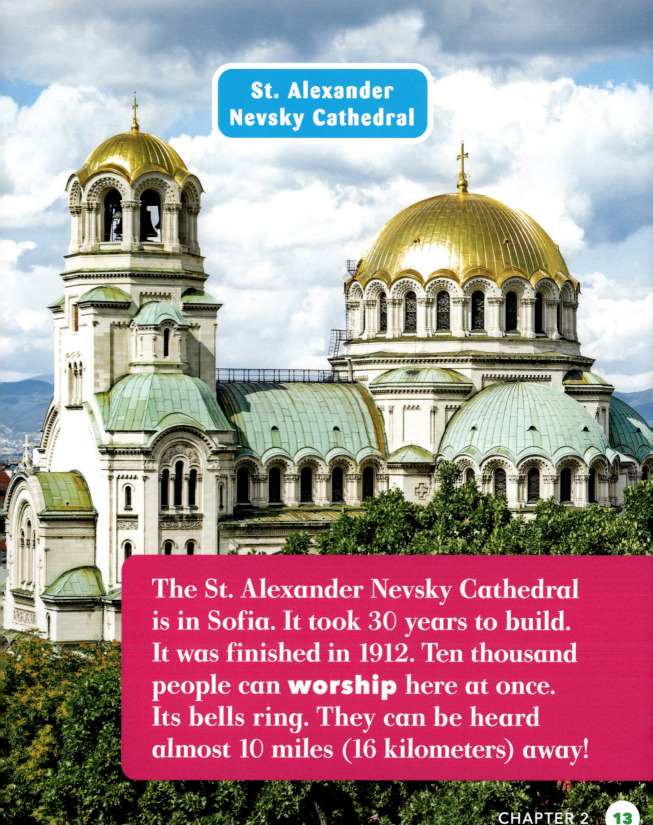

St. Alexander Nevsky Cathedral

The St. Alexander Nevsky Cathedral is in Sofia. It took 30 years to build. It was finished in 1912. Ten thousand people can **worship** here at once. Its bells ring. They can be heard almost 10 miles (16 kilometers) away!

CHAPTER 2

Sofia is the **capital**. Lawmakers meet in the National Assembly Building. The president attends special events. The prime minister leads the government.

Bulgaria is part of the **North Atlantic Treaty Organization (NATO)**. It is also part of the **European Union (EU)**. Both groups help protect the country's freedom.

National Assembly Building

TAKE A LOOK!

Bulgaria's flag has three stripes. What do the colors stand for? Take a look!

☐ = peace, love, freedom
🟩 = farm wealth
🟥 = military courage

CHAPTER 2 15

CHAPTER 3
FOOD AND FUN

People in Bulgaria eat a lot of yogurt. Some say it was invented here 4,000 years ago! It is part of many dishes. Tarator is a yogurt soup. Banitsa is a yogurt and cheese pastry. Musaka is chopped beef and potatoes. It is often topped with a yogurt sauce.

People ski in the Rila Mountains. Musala Peak is here. It is the country's highest point. It is 9,596 feet (2,925 meters) tall.

CHAPTER 3

Baba Marta is a spring holiday. People give one another red and white bracelets. The bracelets stand for health. People wear them until they see the first tree blossoms. Easter and Christmas are also important holidays.

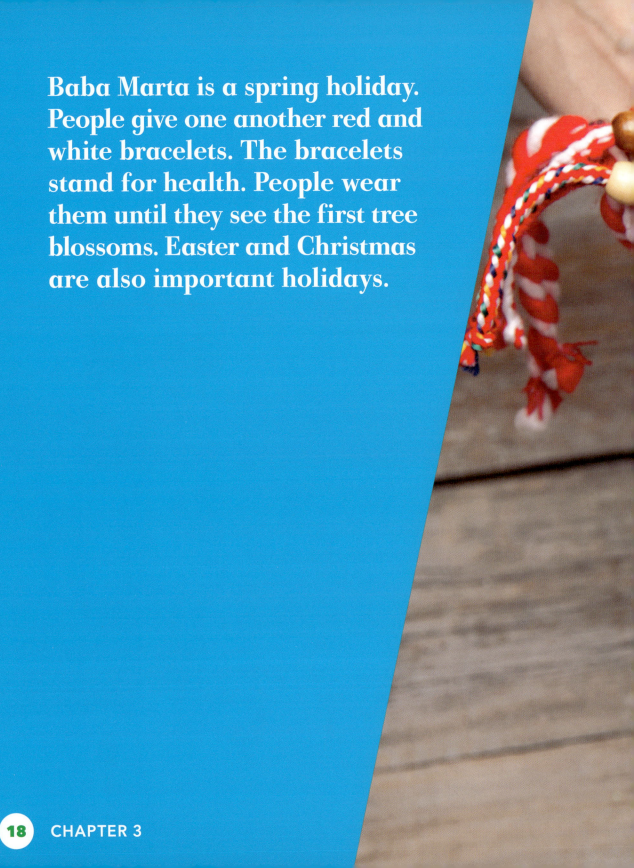

CHAPTER 3

The rose is the national flower. Why? Bulgaria is a top producer of rose oil. There is a rose festival every year. People wear **traditional** clothing.

There is so much to see in Bulgaria! Do you want to visit?

DID YOU KNOW?

It takes more than 3,000 pounds (1,361 kilograms) of rose petals to make two cups (0.5 liters) of oil. The oil is used to make perfume. It helps heal wounds, too!

QUICK FACTS & TOOLS

AT A GLANCE

BULGARIA

Location: southeastern Europe

Size: 42,811 square miles (110,880 square kilometers)

Population: 6,873,253 (2022 estimate)

Capital: Sofia

Type of Government: parliamentary republic

Languages: Bulgarian (official), Turkish, Romani

Exports: petroleum, medicines, copper, wheat

Currency: Bulgarian lev

GLOSSARY

ancient: Belonging to a period long ago.

capital: A city where government leaders meet.

European Union (EU): A group of European countries that have joined together to encourage economic and political cooperation.

fortress: A place that is fortified against attack.

goods: Things that are traded or sold.

North Atlantic Treaty Organization (NATO): An organization of countries that have agreed to give each other military help. This group includes the United States, Canada, and some countries in Europe.

pollution: Harmful materials that damage or contaminate the air, water, and soil.

traditional: Having to do with the customs, beliefs, or activities that are handed down from one generation to the next.

worship: To show love and devotion to a god or gods, especially by praying or going to a religious service.

Bulgaria's currency

QUICK FACTS & TOOLS

INDEX

animals 11
Baba Marta 18
Belogradchik Fortress 4
Black Sea 5, 11
Danube River 7
European Union 14
flag 15
food 16
government 11, 14
Macedonia 7
Musala Peak 17
National Assembly Building 14
national flower 21
Nessebar 5
North Atlantic Treaty Organization 14
Plovdiv 8
Rila Mountains 17
Romania 7
school 12
Serbia 7
ski 17
Sofia 13, 14
St. Alexander Nevsky Cathedral 13
students 12

TO LEARN MORE

Finding more information is as easy as 1, 2, 3.
1. Go to www.factsurfer.com
2. Enter "Bulgaria" into the search box.
3. Choose your book to see a list of websites.